Balboa Press books may be ordered through booksellers or by contacting:

Balboa Press
A Division of Hay House
1663 Liberty Drive
Bloomington, IN 47403
www.balboapress.com
1 (877) 407-4847

ISBN: 978-1-9822-0035-0 (sc)
978-1-9822-0036-7 (e)

Library of Congress Control Number: 2018903458

Print information available on the last page.

Balboa Press rev. date: 09/07/2018

BALBOA.
PRESS
A DIVISION OF HAY HOUSE

12 LOVE NOTES TO MY DAUGHTER

AFFIRMATIONS FOR EACH MONTH OF THE YEAR, BECAUSE LIFE CAN BE ROUGH

LETY MORENO

12 Love Notes to my daughter

An affirmation for each month of the year to create success, even during those difficult moments of each month.

12 Love Notes to my Daughter is a collection of encouraging words to girls and young women inspired by my daughter. They are a copulation of lessons learned, perils of wisdom and words of encouragement to go out and conquer any goal or obstacle that presents through you life. A month to month inspirational series for those moments when life stinks and you think you cannot go on any further. These twelve notes are meant as an encouragement and reminder for every young girl and woman to listen to what they need to hear above the noise of, doubt, shame, low self-esteem, and little confidence. This inner voice full of courage is already within you and if you listen closely, even in those days of doubt, you may hear that inner voice slowly whisper, yes you can.

I too was once a young girl. Your mom and the adult women in your life were young once too. We were women with moments of doubt, fear, frustration, disappointments, heartache, shame, and moments of little confidence in our abilities to do great things in life. We are women who simply decided to listen to that little whisper above the noise that said, yes you can. We can now say yes we did and so can you.

1.   Life is not Always Fair, but do it anyway

"Never dull your shine for someone else."
Tyra Banks

Life is not always fair, we will not always get what we want, sometimes through life you may hear no more than once, but you know what, only the best, only those who tried something new, only those who dare greatly in pursuit of what sets their life in motion ever hear NO. So when you hear no, and you feel you failed at something, know that it's an opportunity to learn, it is a redirection of your life and purpose, it is a time to reflect and evaluate what is important in your life, career and surroundings. Life is not fair, but don't let that stop you, do it anyway.

2. Feel the Fear and do it anyway

"I don't want the fear of failure to stop me from doing what I really care about."
Emma Watson

There are many times you will be afraid, for example, I was afraid when you became part of my world. I wondered if I would be a good enough mother, smart enough, caring enough, compassionate enough. I had doubts and feared messing it all up every step of the way, from the time you took your first steps, to the time you started kinder garden, started to drive a car and went off to college. I felt the fear with every milestone but I did it anyway, many times in your life you will be afraid, you will wonder if you are good enough, smart enough, tall enough, short enough, skinny enough, strong enough, talented enough or prepared enough, and guess what, you wake up, you look in the mirror and you say, "I am good enough, I will do it anyway." Feel the Fear and do it anyway.

3. You are never a victim of circumstances, but you are a product of your reactions and choices

"Society certainly encourages women to be victims in every way"
Gloria Steinem

You will never be prevented from achieving anything you want from this life. You see we are given the same amount of hours every day as the next person, what we choose to do with those hours will define your success in business and life more than anything that comes your way. You may encounter "bad" bosses, bullying, people who don't believe in you, people who are not nice to you even if you are only trying to better yourself, people who are jealous, who are unhappy no matter what you do but if you spend your time giving them your energy you will miss the time you could be creating, studying, living, enjoying life, furthering your education. Do not fall into the trap of blaming and complaining, instead when you find yourself feeling like a victim, reshape and reframe that moment, into productive time and choose to be better. You will never be a victim of circumstances, but you will always be a product of your reaction and choices.

4. I'm only, so I can't

"Women and girls can do whatever they want. There is no limit to what we as women can accomplish."
Michelle Obama

Listen to other people's limitations and you will never know how far you can go. When you hear the word I am only, so I can't, know that these words come from someone who said them somewhere along your lifetime especially when you hear, I am only a girl. See today girls can be scientists, teachers, astronauts, mothers, daughters, they can run companies, be presidents, work in the courtrooms, they can be professionals, doctors, lawyers, singers, actors, artists, professionals, girls can be anything and everything they choose to do. They can be and do anything and everything they set their minds to. When doubt creeps in and you feel like you are not able, remind yourself that I am only, so I CAN.

5.   If I fail it will mean I can't, so why try?

"Failure means a stripping away of the inessential."
J. K. Rowling

In life do me a favor, please expect to fail regardless of how much you prepare. Sometimes life will not be fair, you might not get the promotion, you may not make it to the team you wanted, you may feel inadequate, you might get rejected, you may have a break up, kids may make fun of you and you will feel like it's not worth another try. Expect to fail, because if you don't try regardless of what anybody says or what you may say to yourself, you will need to learn from failure as much as you learn from success, they are both some of the best teachers. Expect to fail, then try again.

6. I'm not Brave or good enough

"We must tell girls their voices are important."
Malala Yousafzai

You are as brave as your first, smallest or biggest failure, it means you tried something new, for those who have never failed have never in reality been brave. The illusion of failure will be more of a disaster than your ability to actually fail at something you do. You cannot call your self brave until you get out there, along with everyone else that is, take the steps necessary to create change, utilize your voice to create the changes you want to see in your life and take the steps necessary regardless of the outcome to create what it is that you want from your life. In those moments that you feel inadequate or not good enough, please call me so I can remind you that you don't need anyone else, you simply need to take the first step in whatever it is that you want to achieve. You are Brave and Good enough.

7.   Believe in Yourself, You deserve it.

"If people are doubting how far you can go, go so far that you can't hear them anymore."
Michele Ruiz

Believe in yourself, it is a gift that requires no permission, entitlement or background. The ability to believe in yourself is not something that requires a birth right, a specific status, it does not come from someone who tells you how to or when, it has no shape, it does not come from material, money or titles, the ability to believe in yourself is something that comes from your ability to define and understand that this is something created and developed from within. Believe in yourself, you deserve that gift.

8.   Find what motivates you

"Do one thing every day that scares you."
– Eleanor Roosevelt

The same thing that motivates you to tell mom no, even if it's what is best for you is the same motivation you already have inside of you. You see, inside of us there is a little voice that tells us what we want to or not want to do. The same voice that gives you courage and makes you brave enough to defy authority or the things in life that may still be good or healthy for you, is the same voice that you need to allow to come through when you need some motivation. When kids say no, there is no other voice in the room, it does not matter if mom says don't do it, or your sister and brother say, you are going to get in trouble or your dad says, I would not do that if I was you. No is okay, well sometimes, it is a way of creating the space you need to define what is important to you. It is okay to say NO at times. It is your center of motivation that creates the courage and the bravery for you to stand up and say NO. Imagine now what would happen if you apply this center of motivation with a calm voice, wisdom, education and choose to defy and create what you really want for your life. Find what motivates you and conquer your biggest fears. You can always call mom so she can tell you NO, you actually can, no excuses.

9. Turn Mountains into Mini Goals

"Too many people quit in life, conquered by the amount of work and steps it will take to achieve, forgetting that it takes a series of steps to arrive at the top of any mountain in business and life."

LetyM

If after reading all these affirmations, going out to school or college and trying to keep up with all the adults in your life, you still feel a little over whelmed, overworked, or stressed out from all the stuff you must get done, I want you to know that parents feel the same way too. So how do parents turn mountains and piles of works, calendars and jobs, bake sales, PTA meetings, exercise, cook lavish meals, wash dishes, do laundry, lunch with friends and still make time to take care of your bobo with a band aide and give you a tissue for your runny nose. Well the secret is to take mini steps to get through any goal, you see there are times when life gets very overwhelming if we allow it to. It is okay to say no sometimes so you can have time for the things you want to say yes to. When you are overwhelmed with homework, housework, jobs and college studies please understand that we understand your stress and concerns. We want you to know that you will be just fine, take the time to divide your work into blocks of time when you can get stuff done and always go after what you desire out of life. You see when you break down your tasks into blocks of productive time the world does not seem so over whelming. Give yourself a check mark or pat in the back every time you achieve something no matter how small and turn your mountains every day into mini goals.

10. Life is not always about change and that is okay

"Be thankful for what you have; you'll end up having more. If you concentrate on what you don't have, you will never, ever have enough."
Oprah Winfrey

In your calendar of life, you may have homework, the time you have to work, when your next outing is even if you don't let mom know, when you are going to party out at the next concert, the next vacation, go to the library, create wonderful and amazing change in the world. I think those are amazing things to do and you should do them. But life is not always about change, it is okay to say I'm okay with the way life is right now. It will give you an opportunity to appreciate life and be thankful for everything you have and everything you already are. I want you to challenge yourself and every day you wake up mention one thing that you are thankful for. You should take the time to pause, celebrate and take time from your busy, world changing, pioneering, rebelling streak and seat back and say, I'm proud of myself, I can sit today, take a minute and be thankful for one thing that is good in my life, call your mom, call your dad or a loved one. Why should you do this? Because if you always want something to change, you will never see that life is also good enough to live, enjoy and celebrate everyday as is with those people already surrounding your life. It is admirable to create change for the better, it is also admirable to appreciate that life is not always about change and that is okay.

11. Own Your Story

> **"If your child marches to a different beat, or a different drummer, you might just have to go along with that music. Help them achieve what is important to them."**
>
> Sonya Sotomayor

Your story is your history, be proud of it and never allow anyone to shame you into thinking you are less than because of who you are or where you came from. Your story is created everyday with your thoughts and choices and I want you to take the time to be proud of who and what you are and represent. Own your story, stand proud on the skirts of your grandmother and mother, stand tall on the heels of your ancestors. Your story is your testimony of how you created your present, how you got here, what motivated you to be who you are today. Own your story with mistakes and successes and be proud of who you are today. Once you accept your failures and success no one can use them against you. Every day you wake up, look in the mirror and say I AM proud of……. And repeat it every day of your life. Your story should never be a weigh on your shoulders, but a spring board to help you achieve. Own Your Story.

12. Define and Be Yourself

"My mother told me to be a lady, and for her that meant be your own person, be independent."
Ruth Bader Ginsburg

Who should you be when you finally grow up? You should be yourself. The road to self discovery is something that is very personal. Mom cannot tell you who to be, dad can't do it for you either, your friends and relatives should not tell you who and what to be, your teachers cannot tell you that either. You and only you alone must decide who you are and what you represent. We may give you suggestions because we have experienced a lot in our life time, we can help guide you, assist you or be there for you, but you must decide who you are and what you stand for. People will tell you who and what you should be, because they love you and some well because they feel like they have to, some may be nice and some not so nice, but none of those people will matter, not even me, because to define your personal happiness and fulfillment you must decide what that means for you and you must be brave enough to accept the consequences of those choices. If you ever make a mistake along the way, hey don't be so tough on yourself, I'll tell you a secret, mom and dad made mistakes too, we were not always perfect and we had to change our definition of what that meant for us as we grew and learned. Define and Be Yourself anyway, I will be here for you every step of the way.

Illustrator's BIO

Lydia Brown was a Sophomore in high school at the time of illustrating. She is from a small town in Illinois and enjoys art, music, and being an active community member. She has hopes of authoring her own story one day.